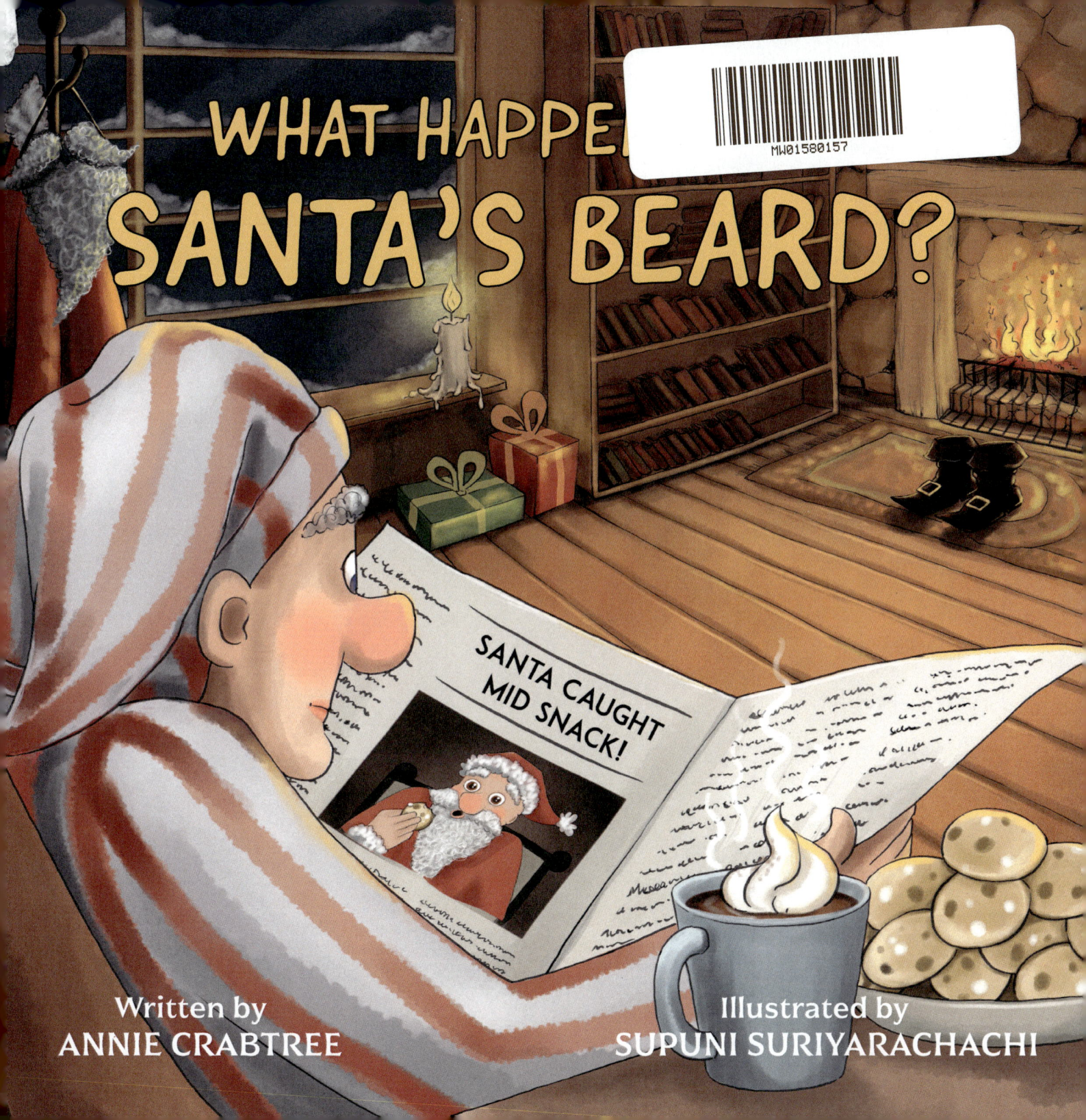

Text © 2020 Annie Crabtree

Illustrations © 2020 Supuni Suriyarachachi

All rights reserved.

No part of this book may be reproduced in any form whatsoever, whether by graphic, visual, electronic, film, microfilm, tape recording, or any other means, without permission of the publisher, except in the case of brief passages embodied in critical reviews and articles.

ISBN 13: 978-1-7360207-0-8

Published by Piggy Tail Tales

Piggy Tail Tales supports O.U.R. and donates 50% of their proceeds to Operation Underground Railroad, helping to save children one book at a time.

Cover design by Supuni Suriyarachachi and Chelsea Jackson

Typeset by Chelsea Jackson

Edited by Chelsea Jackson, Jackson Writing and Editing, LLC

Dedication

To my sweet girls who have helped grow my imagination through Barbie dolls, fort building, and bedtime stories. I love you more than you could ever imagine.

—Mommy

Black shiny boots...
CHECK!

Big red suit...
CHECK!

Fluffy white beard... well, umm, you see....

All right, I know what you're thinking. Who is this guy, and what's he done with the REAL Santa?

It was Christmas Eve, only my third year on the job, and I couldn't wait to get another year under my belt.

Then, it happened.

Or how would little Suzy get her new dolly? And then there's little Jimmy who worked so hard to be good this year. He deserved that new bike!

I needed to think fast. I had exactly 27 minutes and 12 seconds until takeoff. I had to ask for help. I had no choice. I called up my brother, Fred.

Fred had been dying to go out on the route since I started this gig. But unfortunately, he's quite... um... what's a good word? Pokey. He's never been on time in his life. His nickname growing up was "Never Ahead Fred" because he always lagged behind.

In fact, when Fred was a kid, he raced his pet turtle and the turtle won! So, you can see why I hesitated to let him tag along. And now I had to trust him in the driver's seat? What was this world coming to?

Once Fred arrived—late, of course—we had no time to waste. He put on the suit, and I let him do the reindeer send-off.

"On Dasher! On Dancer! On Prancer and Vixen! On Comet! On Cupid! On Donner and Blitzen!"

We shot into the sky.

"Now, Fred, there are three VERY important rules for getting the job done right.

"#1—Always go in through the chimney. If there isn't a chimney, use the door farthest from the bedrooms.

And then Fred faced a rare double-chocolate fudge-filled macadamia nut cookie—our favorite. Our mother made them for us growing up, and it had been years since we'd had one.

While Fred licked the last few crumbs from his fingers, little Anna snuck from her room and snapped a picture with her little pink bunny camera.

Ugh, I knew giving her that camera last year was a mistake.

He popped out of the chimney and told me what had happened.

He broke one of the three rules! Three rules to follow. How hard could it be?

The next day, Fred's picture was all over the news.

Fred was now the face of Santa! Everyone who saw that picture thought HE was the real Santa. Do you know how much harder my job became?

Now that my brother's bearded face was plastered everywhere, I had to give myself a beard or risk disappointing all the kids in the whole wide world.

So, ever since "Beard Bomb," that's what we call that day here at the North Pole, I've had a few close calls. . . .

Oh, and the time I spilled the hot cocoa on my lap.

Last year, I had a family leave me flowers instead of cookies. I have the worst allergies!

And there was that time I forgot the dog treats. . . .

So, the next time you're sitting on Santa's lap and decide to give his beard a little tug...

Just remember—the beard may be fake, but I'm **VERY** real!

About the Author

Annie is a wife, mother of two, personal trainer, yoga instructor, coffee addict, lover of her family and Jesus—and now children's book author! She hopes to make an impact on the world through a little spark of imagination.

Annie has decided to donate 50% of the proceeds from her books to Operation Underground Railroad and help save children through children's books! She wants to bring awareness to O.U.R. and raise money to help fund their mission.

For more information about O.U.R. and the incredible good they do, visit ourrescue.org.

To stay updated on Annie and find other great books for children by Piggy Tail Tales, check out piggytailtales.com.

Made in the USA
Middletown, DE
26 November 2022